Montreal Incentive '92

JAPritchard

MONTREAL

Springtime on Crescent.

*C*orner of St Urbain with Notre-Dame de Montréal (1829) across Place D'Armes.

*P*lace D'Armes, with the city flag and the statue of
de Maisonneuve, who founded Ville-Marie de Montréal in 1642.
Beyond is the old Bank of Montreal Building (remodelled 1905)
with the modern building towering above in the background.

MONTREAL

MICHAEL DRUMMOND
MICHEL TREMBLAY

McClelland & Stewart Inc. Boulton Publishing Toronto

Canadian Cataloguing in Publication Data

Drummond, Michael, 1928–
  Montreal

ISBN 0-7710-2867-9

1. Montréal (Quebec)—Description—Views.
I. Title.

FC2947.37.D78 1990   917.14′28′00222   C90-093450-6
F1054.5.M843D78   1990

Produced by Boulton Publishing Services Inc., Toronto

Design by Fortunato Aglialoro—
Falcom Design and Communications Inc., Toronto.

Printed and bound in Hong Kong by Book Art Inc., Toronto

An infinitesimal fragment of a moment, a click lasting no longer than the blink of an eye or a brief blackout, a trick—perhaps the greatest one of all—played on time of which it's always been said that nothing could stop it, and the soul of a thing or a person is frozen forever. That person is now an image, flattering or not, successful or not, but always faithful and definitive, the record of a precise moment stolen from time and space, an image to be consulted at leisure, to be reproduced, sold or kept secret, a page from a book, or a single word, the "duration" of the person, the thing. The very opposite of eternity, in the service of eternity. Photography.

Now let's take a city, Montreal for example—so beautiful, so many-faceted—and shatter it into a thousand fragments like a mirror that has fallen to the floor, then freeze each splinter into one of those brief blackouts stolen from time. It will reflect images of her inhabitants (local characters and the well-to-do, smiling faces and weeping ones), her monuments (the ones raised to both heroes and gods), the undeniable beauties she's so proud of and the ugly spots she tries in vain to conceal, her timeworn buildings and her neo-something skyscrapers, her moods, her whims, the light that bathes her and the light that emanates from her, the violent orange of her sun as it rises, the ashy rose as it sets. She. In all her splendor. Her abundance.

Each of these fragments will be a complete vision of the city, because each will originate in the same shattered mirror: Parc Lafontaine and Square Saint Louis, the Sun Life Building and the church of Notre-Dame, the fruit-seller and the children behind their schoolyard fence, football players and the barber Gerard Blais, the Port and the painter, Place Ville-Marie and the University, from summer's green to winter's white—all will testify to the singular, the multiple beauties of Montreal. Assembled between the covers of a book they will recreate before our eyes the mirror's polished surface just before it shatters. We will have stolen her soul from Montreal, the better to reproduce it and to celebrate it. By cheating time, destroyer of everything.

MICHEL TREMBLAY
Translated by SHEILA FISCHMAN

Neighbourly shoemaker at the corner of Boulevard St-Laurent and Avenue des Pins East.

Sidewalk artist at work on Rue St Paul West.

The Old Firehall at William and Rue St Pierre, built in 1903 not far from the spot where de Maisonneuve sank the first well in the New World.

Rue St Paul, a busy thoroughfare of Old Montreal, crowded with restaurants and handicrafts.

Architectural details, Rue St Jacques.

Reflective moment at midday.

Banque Nationale de Paris Building on McGill Avenue; Montreal has some of the best new architecture in North America.

Aerial view of the Pont Jacques-Cartier.

Aerial view of the harbour, with Quai King Edward and Quai Jacques Cartier off to the left and the Clocktower on Quai Victoria in the foreground.

*M*any of the stations on the "Metro", Montreal's underground railway, are decorated with impressive works of modern art.

*L*ate afternoon on Tupper; old houses in front of the Maison Mère des Soeurs Grises, with the Canadian Imperial Bank of Commerce Building and Place Ville Marie behind.

Saturday morning, Atwater Market.

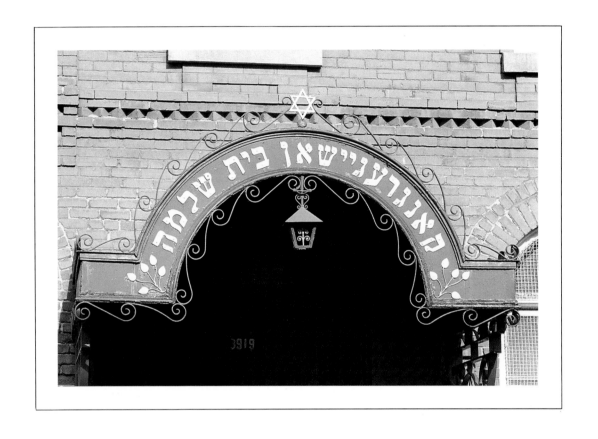

Synagogue doorway at Clark and Bagg.

Montreal has a long established Hasidic community.

*T*he biggest in Canada when constructed in 1914, the Sun Life
Building stored much of Britain's bullion reserves in the
Second World War.

*T*raditional lace graces a doorway on Colonial Street.

*Afternoon on Rue St Paul; the former Hotel Rasco where
Charles Dickens once lodged.*

*Children playing round the George Etienne Cartier Monument,
Parc Mont-Royal.*

Decorated balcony in traditional Quebec style.

Portuguese café on Duluth.

Kindergarten children, Rue St Urbain.

Gateway to Chinatown, Rue de la Gauchetière.

Mural on Laval.

Neighbourhood barbershop—a city tradition.

Residential row on Sherbrooke, converted to professional offices.

Early morning sunlight on the Hôtel de Ville, with the flags of Quebec, Canada and the City of Montreal.

Old Montreal from Île Ste-Hélène, with the white dome of the Old Courthouse (1857), the green roofs of the Hôtel de Ville (1857) and the dome of the Marché Bonsecours (1845).

Classical statuary on Boulevard René Lévesque, seen against the background of Place Ville Marie.

Looking up at the Aldred Building from Place d'Armes.

Parc Mont-Royal—five hundred acres of beautiful woodland overlooking the city.

Notre-Dame from Île Ste-Hélène with the Aldred Building and the Maison des Coopérants.

Christchurch Anglican Cathedral and the Maison des Coopérants (1988), commonly known as "the Cathedral Building".

Antique mail-box on Crescent.

The statues atop the Cathedral-Basilica of Mary, Queen of the World, portray the patron saints of the archdiocese.

Autumnal colouring, Rue Anderson.

Bookshop on Sherbrooke.

Place Jacques-Cartier, the centre point of Old Montreal, was first opened as a city market in 1804.

Place Jacques-Cartier.

Southeast prospect in the fall from the Mount Royal lookout.

Rue Laval, part of the "old village" of Montreal.

Avenue Henri-Julien, off St-Denis.

Westmount City Hall on Christmas Eve.

Early morning in winter on Quai Jacques-Cartier.

Snow blankets the Old Fire Hall, Rue St Pierre and Prince William.

Rue St Paul under snow, looking towards the Chapel of Notre-Dame-de-Bonsecours (1886–1892).

Skating on Rue de la Commune in winter.

Rue de la Commune in spring.

Christmas decorations outside the Ritz Carlton Hotel, at Drummond and Sherbrooke.

A child's enchanted world; watching the animated toys in the windows of Ogilvy's at Christmas.

Furs on a bright, cold January day.

*Trafalgar apartment building on Chemin de la Côte-des-Neiges,
seen from Hill Park Road.*

Snowstorm on Rue de la Commune looking west.

Snowstorm on Rue de la Commune looking east.

Tower of the University of Montreal seen from the Cemetery of Notre-Dame-des-Neiges.

*C*hurch domes, City of Lachine. The name comes from the estate
given to the great explorer La Salle (1643-1687) and refers to his
dream that in New France he would discover the route to China.

Playing hockey in Sir George Etienne Cartier park in St Henri.

Cross-country skier on top of Mount Royal.

The harbour in winter, with Notre-Dame and the Hôtel de Ville.

*The harbour in winter with Marché Bonsecours (1845), for many
years the principal market for food in the city.*

Details of a calèche.

*Olympic Stadium, Maisonneuve Park, home of the 1976 games;
the Stadium can accommodate more than 70,000 people.*

Bean jars at Marché Jean-Talon.

*Artist on Rue St Amable, a street of old Montreal that is a focal
point for painters, jewellers and local crafts.*

Hardware store on Boulevard St-Laurent, "The Main", the east-west dividing street or meridian of the city, one of the most diverse and fascinating stretches in all of Montreal.

Corner grocery store with delivery bicycles, Avenue de Gaspé.

Monument in the Cemetery of Notre-Dame-des-Neiges.

"Cabanes" for ice fishing on Lac St Louis, a centuries-old winter quest for muskie, doré, perch and pike, or whatever else the hidden waters afford.

Bank of Montreal Building (1905) and Rue St Jacques in winter.

Presbytery of Notre-Dame de Montréal.

Ice-boating on Lac St Louis—a sport of great and growing popularity.

Sledding in Parc Mont-Royal.

Dorchester Square, with the Anglican church of St George.

Winter woods near Beaver Lake, Parc Mont-Royal.

Cemetery of Notre-Dame-des-Neiges, with the Oratory in the distance.

*St Joseph's Oratory (1924–1955) seen from Westmount Mountain;
one of the most visited Catholic shrines in the world, this is the only
major place of pilgrimage dedicated to the patron saint of healing.*

Busy morning at a pastry stall, Boulevard St-Laurent.

Mother and child, Rue Jeanne Mance.

Sleigh-ride in Parc Mont-Royal.

*Once the principal means of winter transport throughout the city,
a sleigh-ride is now simply a source of enjoyment that brings a
smile on a snowy day.*

St George's Anglican church, opposite Windsor Station.

1981 McGill College Avenue.

Old Westmount houses.

Midwinter stroll on Place Jacques-Cartier.

Montreal is host to visitors from every part of the world.

Aerial view of downtown from over the harbour.

A game of pétanque in Parc La Fontaine.

Lawn bowling, Westmount.

Feeding the pigeons on Boulevard St-Laurent.

Fountain in Square St-Louis.

International bicycle-race passes along Sherbrooke West.

Loading freight in the harbour.

A pause for refreshment in Chinatown.

La Galérie du Néon, Boulevard St-Laurent.

Alliance Building, Sherbrooke West.

Calèche on Place d'Armes, in front of Notre-Dame.

*S*pire of Notre-Dame-de-Bonsecours, (1886–1892). This lovely
little church on the old harbour is affectionately known as the
"sailors' church"; model ships hang from the ceiling.

*T*o the right of Marché Bonsecours may be seen the great statue of
the Virgin that stands above the Chapel of Notre-Dame-de-
Bonsecours, arms outstretched to the harbour.

*Cathedral-Basilica of Mary Queen of the World and Saint James
the Greater, built between 1870 and 1894 as an exact scale model of
St Peter's in Rome.*

Bandstand in Parc Mont-Royal.

*P*lace Victoria, the new Montreal.

*M*ontreal Pool Room Restaurant, Boulevard St-Laurent.

Crescent Street.

Place Montreal Trust.

City at night from the Pont de la Concorde.

Marché Bonsecours and the old waterfront by night.

Portrait from a music festival, Parc Mont-Royal.

Preparation for a children's festival, Boulevard St-Laurent.

Eggs at Atwater Market.

Eggs at Marché Jean-Talon.

Montreal from Île St-Hélène.

Wellington Street, Verdun.

Square St Louis.

Rachel and De Mentana.

*A*ntiques store on Crescent.

*A*nnual street festival, Boulevard St-Laurent.

*McGill University campus; opened in 1828, the university is one
of the premier homes of learning on the continent.*

Late autumn, Parc Mont Royal.

Clock of the Hôtel de Ville.

Hôtel de Ville with the Nelson Column (1809).

Clouds reflected on Sherbrooke West.

Rue Notre-Dame West.

Entrance to Notre-Dame.

*Musée des Beaux-Arts de Montréal on Sherbrooke, the oldest
museum in Canada, established in 1912.*

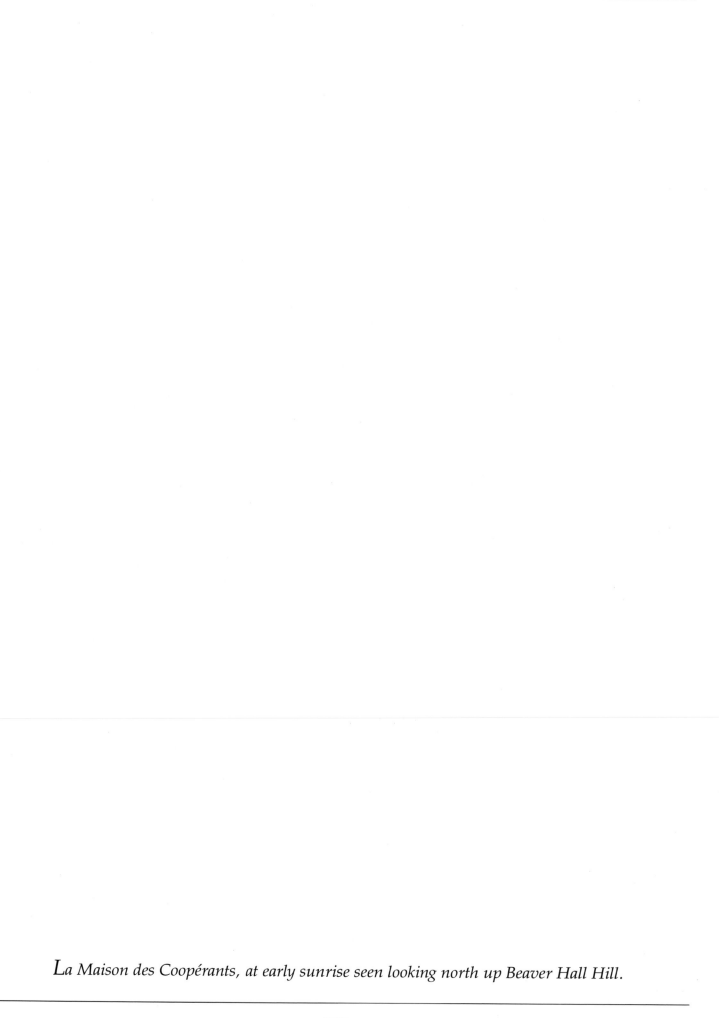

La Maison des Coopérants, at early sunrise seen looking north up Beaver Hall Hill.

Sunrise from Mount Royal.

A quiet evening at the Restaurant le Parchemin, on University.

Interior of Notre-Dame de Montréal (1829), designed by Victor Bourgeau.

"Temperance" and "Perseverance", the twin towers of Notre-Dame de Montréal.